ERASE

ENDURE

ERASE
ENDURE

POEMS

Joel Thomas Katz

DUTCH POET PRESS
2020

Copyright © 2020 Joel Thomas Katz
and Dutch Poet Press
All Rights Reserved.

ISBN Number 978-1-7342742-0-2

Dutch Poet Press
dutchpoetpress.com

Acknowledgments

The Dorothea Lasky epigraph is a phrase from the poem "The Secret Life of Mary Crow" in her book *Milk* (2018) with permission of the publisher Wave Books.

The Mary Ruefle epigraph on page 23 is used with the permission of the author.

The phrase on page 29 is excerpted from the poem "What It Was" by Mark Strand in his book *Blizzard of One* (1988) with permission of the publisher Alfred A. Knopf, Inc.

An earlier version of "Namesakes" on page 33 appeared previously in *spring mother tongue: Poetic Voices of Santa Clara County*, lulu.com, 2017.

Collage material of the Yom Kippur prayer *Ki Hiney ka-Khomer* for the front cover is taken from *Mahzor Lev Shalem for Rosh Hashanah and Yom Kippur*, The Rabbinical Assembly, Inc., 2010, page 227.

Many thanks to the following people for comments on earlier versions of various poems: Kathryn Abelson, Jane Jacobson, Esther Kamkar, Joy Katz, Jane Miller and the Belvedere poets, Robert Perry. Also to Jessica Nielsen for her diligent proofreading.

For my father Daniel B. Katz

CONTENTS

ERASE

- 5 First Halloween After 9/11
- 6 *The Authoritative Life of General William Booth*
- 7 *The Melting of Molly*
- 8 Aquarium
- 9 *The Actress in High Life*
- 10 First Thing
- 11 *The Land of Little Rain*
- 12 *History of the Gatling Gun Detachment*
- 13 Midway
- 14 *Pointed Roofs*
- 15 *Happiness and Marriage*
- 16 *Clouds*
- 17 Looking at an Eric Fischl Painting, I Recall What a Neighbor Said

ENDURE

- 21 Night
- 22 Song of the Glass
- 23 Response to Mary Ruefle
- 24 Swerve
- 26 Blessing the People
- 28 These are the New Rituals
- 29 On a Phrase of Mark Strand
- 30 Waiting
- 31 Melisma
- 33 Namesakes
- 34 Traces of You
- 35 Two Vineyards
- 36 Traveler
- 37 Long Lines
- 38 The One

POSTSCRIPT
41   Disassembling
42   Gerbil
43   First Father's Day Without
44   The Eggs
45   Pockets
46   New Life

NOTE to the Reader

Some of the poems under ERASE in the first section of the book were created thanks to the Wave Books website erasures.wavepoetry.com. The software transforms passages from selected works of fiction and non-fiction, revealing "the hidden poem within."

Here are public domain source texts supplied by the website upon which the author performed the erasures:

"The Authoritative Life of General William Booth" by G.S. Railton. General William Booth (1829-1912) was the founder of the Salvation Army.

"The Melting of Molly" by Maria Thompson Davies

"The Actress in High Life" by Sue Petigru Brown

"The Land of Little Rain" by Mary Austin

"History of the Gatling Gun Detachment" by John Henry Parker

"Pointed Roofs" by Dorothy Miller Richardson

"Happiness and Marriage" by Elizabeth Towne

"Clouds" by Aristophanes

Thinning and thickening are both part of a painting.

—Attributed to Robert Rauschenberg

I know the body is a corpse and text
But is also a possibility

—Dorothea Lasky

ERASE

First Halloween After 9/11

They come to the door dressed as
firemen, police, rescue workers
with hard hats. They ring the bell
and stand there; no one chants
trick or treat. To those without
special costume we ask
Who are you? And they answer, smiling,
the passengers. All that candy
we bought for handouts now so
useless. Instead, we find ourselves
taking their hands, telling them
Thank you … Thank you …

The Authoritative Life of General William Booth

              lead on   in so vast a
territory

                                    God
                    periodically passed through

                            such solitary
spheres yield to discouragement

The Melting of Molly

    I wasn't twenty and

said

        God didn't want to see me   trotting along slow and
tired   pounds and pounds of
plumpness
        I feel   He is going to

                    put me out

                          chastening my spirit

      hovering even to the third and fourth generation

Aquarium

After September 11th the two of them decided to try small things instead. They bought an aquarium with porcelain figurines of a deep-sea diver and mini treasure chest, then spread gravel along the bottom in neat rows of red-white-and-blue. But two mornings later, when he found the scooter blenny floating on its side, she took a hammer to the tank and buried the smithereens in the garden. Then she turned to him and muttered *I'm not ready to have kids*.

The Actress in High Life

      a busy scene   in Elvas

Asses
about the square, each with his nose tied up in a net, that he might not eat his saddle

peasants   mingling with the

                              pig merchant, with
his   ear-piercing merchandise

                    peasant women
persuasively offering for sale

a monk   and   friars aplenty And here in the midst of

              the lounging citizens of Elvas

                  a spark   would at times
shine out from them

First Thing

My friend had a mild case of glaucoma in both eyes. The clinic recently performed surgery on one of them.

Today she told me how she goes outside first thing in the morning to enjoy the sky: she holds one eye shut, then the other, alternating—she likes the way the sky becomes yellow ... blue ... yellow ... blue ...

The Land of Little Rain

       the nature of   hills, rounded

blunt, burned, squeezed up out of

valleys
        and

                            pure desertness

rimmed   with

                hummocks

                            quick

storms

         edges   at
              which

                  to find springs, but

not   depend upon them

Here

                  Here

          the tilted   dust
     whirling   Here

                         with little

in it to love

History of the Gatling Gun Detachment

        there is a box   on fire!

           Let's throw it into the river

                the smoke was still ascending

      throw the box in the river   in the water
        the blue smoke continued to bubble up

Midway

Then the ferry between Seattle and Bainbridge Island stopped midway: "Just a few minutes for a brief memorial service," announced the captain. The lower deck of 72 cars and 15 motorcycles stood at attention, and the passengers above imagined unseen fragments powdering the bay … three blasts of the ferry's horn and the boat's engines rumbled back to life. One passenger thought *those blasts were the person's final request.*

Pointed Roofs

The   bright   plentiful mirrors, the long sweep
of   faces
scattered here

    the   music

                                                         she
could not see whether they were lines or spaces

                                    her fingers
    stiffened and she   worked them from her elbows like
sticks

dreadful movements   She   heard
nothing
    but

       the   red-hot mass of   fire

                 the room   full of
stupid people who had made her play

          the notes   fumbled and slurred

Happiness and Marriage

All this   judgment   is simply

                                  for and against,
      waiting   to decide

                                  Just be still and

  think through
    the other side of things

Clouds

                                              the Moon
            commanded us

                  dreadful things, though
           not in words

                                      torches
                 went out

            beautiful   she says
                   you
                confuse   up and down
            gods are constantly
          defrauded

                                you ought to be
sacrificing

and laughing   For

           gods
will know better   the days of
         the Moon

**Looking at an Eric Fischl Painting,
I Recall What a Neighbor Said**

"It's pretty dark for a midnight."

(as if there were degrees of empty)

ENDURE

Night

This is the swirl that night offers, this is the feta you crumble
over your roasted sweet potatoes, this is the young wine
you prefer to a glass of Aged-Seven-Years, these are the hours
that confound and cling to your skin like the salt of an absent lover.
The moon, the yard with its fence leaning in spots, rotting in others,
a neighbor's dog yipping its brusque arias. The redwood
towering over the Japanese maple like the memory of your father's
arm around your shoulders until that fleeting weight recedes,
then there's just the dull rumble of a medevac copter above.
Here is the noun, there is the verb—all in a night's work:
someone is busy explaining it all in a language laced with crickets.

Song of the Glass

Not half empty or half full
but what we lift to our lips

over the hasty clutter of breakfast.
Yet how can a liquid

contain a liquid?—I'm thinking of
Old Boston colonial windows,

their purpled panes thicker at the bottom
because liquids flow downhill—

Then there's the beach at nearby
Mattapoisett: enough silica
for an entire city of windows.

The ocean there seldom looks
like a sheet of grey glass:

foam-caps, small churnings.
It hurts so much

to run through the icy waves.
We stroll the beach instead,

dragging our toes through the grains—
like us, so numerous and fine.

Response to Mary Ruefle

*"Pity the slow passage
from the soul to the esophagus"*

Long way down
chants the crew of Her Majesty's frigate,
lowering the mainsail.

Long way down
sings the hard-hat on the nest of beams
atop the unfinished skyscraper
as he opens his lunch pail.

Long way down
mumbles the crisis specialist
before addressing the woman on the ledge
through a bullhorn.

Long way down
croons the janitor as he
lowers the flag in front of the junior high.

Long way down
prays the astronaut before
entering the earth's atmosphere.

Long way down
sings the penny dropped into the well.

Swerve

In the Annals of Whátever
is written what will become of me—
that volume has not yet been
published, still awaits editors
to finish all their crossings-out.
In various margins some have written
Swerve! as if commanding a car
skidding on a rain-slick street
to avoid hitting the pedestrian. Plus
they're so enamored of their own words
they turn the paper over, holding it
up to the light, viewing the backward
handwriting then saying
"Such loops! All that nervous
energy channeled into jaggedness!
The verve of the dotted i ... !" Meanwhile
the toast is burning (mine, not theirs),
morning is sliding its lazy feet
across the kitchen linoleum.
Swerve! they tell me. Too late.
Too late: I've already hit
upon the reason why grass is green
instead of purple, why people
do what they do instead of listening
to the Poobahs of Whátever.
In the background, a radio announces
the latest rock band: Nacho Picasso.
When you look at a painting, where
do your eyes land? Better, when you hear
the city, where do your ears land?
I heard of a novelist who
stopped writing at age seventy.

When asked about it, he said *I have*
the words but not the sentences.
Which is not quite my problem.
A slice of toast and green tea:
that's how to begin the day.
Meanwhile, morning is illumining
the pile of dishes, the granite counters.
In order to avoid getting hit
by lightning, stay indoors, stay
a coward. Or else be as generous
as filling a toaster with diamonds. Be
as open as a banana peel.
No matter what people say, I turn
my ear inward to a distant broadcast.
These days I tell my friends
to swerve, swerve & go jagged.

Blessing the People

*The Lord spoke to Moses: Tell Aaron and his sons
thus shall ye bless the people of Israel:*
   *May the Lord bless you and protect you.
   May the light of His countenance shine upon you
      and be gracious unto you.
   May He lift His face unto you and grant you peace.*
      —Numbers 6:22-26

The ceremony starts with a row of us up front,
descendants of Aaron the Priest facing the Holy Ark
and its Torah scrolls, our backs to the congregation.
We lift our prayer shawls over our heads
then turn around and face the worshippers.
Under my tallis I extend my arms toward them,
fingers spread in a pattern
that inspired Spock's Vulcan salute on Star Trek.
I cannot see them through the wool of my tallis;
they're supposed to be looking away from us—
everyone shielded from the Divine Presence, the *Shekhina*,
which is now presumably descending. The cantor chants
each word of the Priestly Blessing in an undertone,
like a musical cue card, then we sing each word
to a thousand-year-old melody.
It's at this point on a particular Yom Kippur
that a bee flies up under my tallis.
But I'm not about to break decorum.
Actually, I'm smiling: will the congregation
still be there when I remove my tallis?
Like the kid they tell *Close your eyes
and make a wish*, then blow out the candles.

The kid gathers a lungful of air, expels, then opens
his eyes, hoping the classmates have disappeared.
Can I really bless *all* of this congregation,
knowing some of them as I do?
My grandfather, who died before I was born,
refused to perform this ceremony, claimed
he was unworthy. My mind is wandering …
I'm supposed to be focused, be a vessel.
The bee has disappeared. Then the unknown voice
of my grandfather reaches me:
Who are you to judge? Just do it,
do the thing I was unable to do.

These are the New Rituals

after donning skates at the rink, bow
down to the ice to honor its stubbornness

shake together pepper, sugar and baby powder
to form a bounded cloud

wave some fig leaves over a bowl of rice

sing your lover's name while inhaling

close your fist around water to retain its curve

bow again

On a Phrase of Mark Strand

It was the beginning of a chair, not yet legs or cushion,
just an urge to become a place, a pause,
the hint of a refrain. It was the beginning of a day
where awnings unfurled, shops opened and bargains
got snapped up, a day on which a fence
would get blown down to reveal what hadn't occurred
to anyone while they stood there waiting
for the first snow. There was a day and a chair
but not just yet, the way one thinks
"a brick and a brick and finally a house."
How easy it is to be a chair:
roped webbing of the seat and back,
fibers of twisted filaments, each strand
a thought linking one possibility to another
until at last there's a chair, a place, an impulse,
a refrain.

Waiting

gym can wait exercise can wait the waiter waits
for us to choose appetizers and a main delicacy
after waiting the check finally arrives the chick
pecks its way out of the egg out of the relic
of waiting to be born to be freed to be fed
to grow into a chicken and wind up as vindaloo
o we can hardly wait to swallow all that goodness

Melisma

[singing a single syllable of text while moving between several different notes]

Melting snow sliding down the roof

A frown lengthening

Scent of the marsh at high tide, then at low

Running the tongue along the backs of bottom teeth

The mewing of gulls

In Paris: the chocolate's citrus after-hint from the Madagascar soil of the cacao beans

Henry's uni-brow

In the parking lot: a silver Camry next to a silver Corolla next to a silver Prius

Yawn circling the conference room

Glassblower's encased breath as the liquid undulates and cools

The Susquehanna flowing over reeds, the occasional tire, a shopping cart

My slide from 59 to 60

Ten-pins scattered & reset, scattered & reset—ten times this happens to me, then once again ten times

The entire month after my mother died

Namesakes

So I wondered about my namesake and opened a Bible
to the Book of Joel (minor prophet, just three chapters)
and found locusts—a plague of them—laying waste the vines,
splintering fig trees and stripping the bark,
covering the moon with a rusty gauze.
And nobody was standing around with hands on hips,
shaking their heads in tight circles of annoyance,
going "Locusts. *Locusts.* Can you believe it?"
No, they were abject and repentant. And Joel declared
*Sound the trumpet, solemnize a fast, proclaim an assembly
and cry out to the Lord.*
　　　　　　　　I couldn't be that Joel.
I'd rather be my other namesake—*Yosef* in Hebrew,
Joseph: braggart to his brothers, dreamer,
sold to a passing caravan and thrown into prison
from which Pharaoh would pluck him to decode
the nightmarish seven fat cows and seven lean cows.
And Joseph goes on to save the citizens from seven years of
famine—now that's a namesake!
　　　　　　　　Then there's me with a mortgage,
a dented car and a failed lawn, someone who can mutter
helpful facts like

　　the opposite faces of dice total to seven

　　when people argue, it sounds better in Italian

　　a tree stripped of its bark is still a tree

and needs to turn for solace to the ancient Joel, who said
So rend your heart and not your garments.

Traces of You

Horses in the far field pounding the grasses flat

I gather the crumbs and press them back into toast

Here is the chocolate rum-cake, ready to plunge into

Grove of peeling eucalyptus (faint smell of mint)

Cloud-shadows gliding over wheat field and baseball diamond and strip mall

Here is a positron heading towards collision

You can shout your way through the clouds

Yellow plastic mini-silos at the freeway exit that buckle on impact

Two Vineyards

So they sent the Chief Worrier, Yoash ben Yaakov, out to the fields, into the vineyards of King Solomon. There were questions to consider: Would the rains come in their due season? Would they come at all? Would the kingdom be rent by family squabbling?

Yoash thought: for all of Solomon's wisdom, the king is a lot like his father King David—the number of women, the way the Queen of Sheba was captivated by him. After David did not get to build the Holy Temple, Solomon set about the task with taxes and forced labor and timbers from Lebanon, copper and other metals from the desert mines at Timna. What would people in the future make of all this stubborn energy? What else was there to worry about?

So they sent the Chief Worrier out to the fields where words like *tiroir, microclimate* and *malolactal* hold sway. Her work shirt did not reveal her name (Cindy Robertson, Winemaker). They asked her to assess the particulars: brix content of the grapes, organic fertilizer, play of temperature and wind pattern. Not to mention how a given variety of grape might meld with barrels of French as opposed to American oak.

She thought: Are there any hints of coming insect infestation? For all the lab beakers and vine-yield software, how to engineer a certain percentage of alcohol into the fermentation process? After all that science, it's still an art, a place for intuition and the unknowable. And all you can do is wait: from the planting to the winter dormancy to the spring pruning to the summer crush. There's still room for the word *pray.*

Traveler

(on Southwest flight #136, San Jose to Portland)

There is no end to the parade of women at the airport,
some dashing to their gate, breathless   and what of
the woman at O'Hare I heard about years ago,
how her hands extended under the lavatory faucet
failed to trip the electronic sensor (her chemo)

—did she storm out of the bathroom, re-enter
the security area with pennies stuffed in her shoes
and set off the screening device, shouting
I am **here**   *I am* **here**

Right now I'm in the air myself, struggling
to open a packet of honey-roasted peanuts
that all are granted along with Mt. Shasta below
in the last inches of daylight   moments like

the one I finally became an orphan and everything
dissolved: all those women rushing to the gate
and the men and the children …
then my jaw softened and I considered
the body I was falling back into.

Long Lines

I wanted the sweep of them to enter my poems,
so I sought out supermarkets at 6 pm, banks on Fridays:
that some length would seep into me
but not the waiting. Where else to look?
—jet contrails leaching out, spine of the Continental Divide,
single breath of a nylon line cast onto the blank stream,
hoping for fish. And at the edge of the continent
the waves, the waves: incoming, breaking, some of them
reaching shore.

The One

I'll wind up being the one who removes the locks
from a narrow bridge just downstream of Notre Dame Cathedral,
the "love locks" that couples have clamped to the grillwork
in their enthusiasm: locks attached over other locks
until the sides of the bridge are sagging forests of metal.
The City Fathers have spoken. And I must carry this out
in the middle of the night, for who would want to see tokens of
undying love dismembered?

I'll wind up being the one who removes the slips of paper
from the crevices of the *Kotel*: massive stone-wall remnant
of the Holy Temple in Jerusalem. By tradition I am
not permitted to read the folded notes of petition, prayer.
Instead I will pluck them out in the middle of the night
and bury them the next day on the nearby Mount of Olives
which faces the Old City's sealed *Gate of Mercy*,
through which the Messiah will enter Jerusalem in the future.

I want to be the one who undoes each of your padlocks,
who buries all your petitions.

I'll wind up being the one who breaks your heart.

POSTSCRIPT

Daniel B. Katz (1922-2018), *zikhrono li'vrakha*

Disassembling

Take this divot, for instance, on a fairway
overlooking Golden Gate Bridge:

some golfer overcome by
all that red-orange beauty

who forgot to replace
the turf chunk we are now hiking past

though from July through October
the nearby foghorns groan

more than five hours a day
bridge cloaked in mist

so maybe the golfer
was distracted by something else

something mundane
perhaps the thought of his father

recovering from hip surgery.
O my love, why have we

never been lured by golf
with its myriad clubs and irons, shoes and sweaters

choosing instead to hike these seaside hills,
seduced by each other?

Gerbil

One summer day between high school and college, I was helping my dad clean out the garage. To pass the time, we decided to think of song lyrics whose key word could be replaced with the word *gerbil*. (We used to have pet gerbils.)

Let's see, there's

> Oh the yellow rose of Gerbil …

> Gerbil in the morning, gerbil in the evening, gerbil at suppertime …

> I'm dreaming of a White Gerbil …

> I'll be with you in gerbil-blossom time …

> Some enchanted gerbil …

> The rain in Spain falls mainly on the gerbils …

And the winner:

> The hills are alive with the sound of gerbils …

First Father's Day Without

A friend asks *Which is heavier: a pound of feathers or a pound of lead
or the mourner's black ribbon you wore and tore at the cemetery
and which now hangs from a corkboard in your man-cave?*

In morning's brightening light:
each bird-caw the syllable of some future poem,
clouds cryptic as his handwritten scrawls.

A friend says *It's time to shuffle and re-deal.*

A friend asks *If you start out from point A on a train
traveling 80 miles an hour, how long will it take before
your father appears in a dream?*

Next available dream: in the clearing, a circle of ten foxes
facing inward, waiting for someone to happen.

For now, I'm folding the dough
into a loaf I might fathom.

The Eggs

A limousine takes seven of us back from the cemetery to the housing complex. My eleven-year-old nephew Chance is thrilled to be riding in a limo, as if we were going to a prom he will later experience. We gather in the Commons room for the "Meal of Consolation" as my father called it thirteen years earlier when my mother died. There are trays of salads, pasta, pita & hummus, deli …

Toward the end of the meal and conversation, my brother discovers the trayful of thirty hard-boiled eggs, traditional food after a funeral: closed and solid like a mouth shut and struck dumb. Wait! … Weren't we supposed to *start* the meal with the eggs? Did we do it all wrong? Did we need to restart the funeral?

Pockets

The rabbi is saying: Before the deceased is buried, it is traditional for the body to undergo *taharah*, a solemn ritual washing, after which the body is clothed in a simple linen shroud without pockets. One leaves the way one entered —bearing nothing.

New Life

In a Jewish custom called *Shloshim*, male mourners refrain from shaving during the thirty days after the death of a parent or spouse. The unkempt look signals the mourner's status, suggesting that he is focusing on the deceased rather than on his own appearance.

On Day 31 after my dad's funeral, I walk into a traditional barber shop in downtown Bozeman run by two thirty-somethings in baseball caps: Kyle brim-forward and Cody brim-backward and a hefty beard.

After preliminary thinning with an electric shaver, Cody leans me back in the chair, places a warm towel over my face to soften the skin, then applies the heated lather. Next, an attentive straight-razor shave, followed by a cool towel to reinstate skin moisture.

The whole procedure takes forty minutes. Cody then sits me up and turns the chair toward the mirror. Running my fingers along the lower face, I say "Smooth as a baby's tush."

"Yup" says Kyle, "it's like starting a new life."

COLOPHON

Cover and Interior Design by Robert Perry
Dutch Poet Press, Palo Alto, California

Printed and Bound by IngramSpark

Typefaces
Display: Museo Slab
Text: Avenir Next

Notes from Robert Perry

For the cover design, I made an encaustic oil painting with collage intended to reflect the resonant themes of *Erase* and *Endure* found in this book dedicated to the poet's father Daniel B. Katz.

When I first read Joel's poems for the book, the vision for the cover came to me instantly. I knew right then I wanted to represent visually what Joel conveyed—the ongoing effort of humankind to reconcile the opposing forces of *Erase* and *Endure*. I tried to depict that struggle of experiencing erasure and learning endurance toward a greater good with its inevitable successes and failures.

I asked Joel to choose a fitting text in Hebrew for the collage that is seen emerging from the wax in the painting. Joel selected *Ki Hiney ka-Khomer*, his father's favorite prayer from the Yom Kippur service. Along with Rosh Hashanah, Yom Kippur is dedicated to reconciliation and transformation. Duly inspired and grateful, I strove to capture in the painting a sense of those poignant and hopeful aspirations that Joel expressed so tellingly in his extraordinary poems.

www.ingramcontent.com/pod-product-compliance
Lightning Source LLC
Chambersburg PA
CBHW071035080526
44587CB00015B/2632